The Masque of the Red Death

Plague, Privilege & Inevitable Doom
Behind Locked Castle Walls

A Modern Translation
Adapted for the Contemporary Reader

Edgar Allan Poe

Translated by Tim Zengerink

Table of Contents

Preface
Message to the Reader

Rebuilding the Greatest Library in Human History

Thousands of years ago, the Library of Alexandria was the heart of global knowledge — a sanctuary where the wisdom of every known civilization was gathered and shared freely.

And then, it was lost.

Now, we're rebuilding it — and you are invited to join us.

At the Library of Alexandria, we've set out to make every book available to every person on Earth — not just in print, but in every language, every format, and for every reader.

Here's how we do it:

- **Deluxe Print Editions at True Printing Cost** - Order any book as a high-quality paperback, elegant hardcover, or stunning boxset — and only pay what it costs to print. No markups. No middlemen.
- **Unlimited Access to the Greatest Works** - Enjoy thousands of timeless classics — from Plato to Shakespeare to Tolstoy — in beautiful, modern eBook and audiobook editions. Read and listen without limits — for every reader, everywhere.
- **Modern Translations for Every Language & Dialect** - We're reimagining the classics in clear, accessible language — and translating them into every dialect imaginable. Everyone deserves to understand humanity's greatest ideas.

When you visit **LibraryofAlexandria.com**, you're not just accessing books — you're joining a global movement to restore, preserve, and share the wisdom of civilization.

Join us today at LibraryofAlexandria.com

Together, we'll ensure the light of human wisdom never fades again.

With gratitude,

The Modern Library of Alexandria Team

Visit:
www.libraryofalexandria.com
Or scan the code below:

1

Introduction

Poe's Vision of Mortality and
the Gothic Landscape

Edgar Allan Poe's *The Masque of the Red Death* (1842) stands as one of his most iconic and allegorical tales, a masterpiece of Gothic imagery, psychological intensity, and philosophical depth. Set during a time of a devastating plague known as the "Red Death," the story focuses on Prince Prospero, who attempts to defy the inevitable force of death by secluding himself and a group of courtiers inside an opulent, fortified abbey. Within its walls, they indulge in lavish masquerade balls, oblivious—or willfully ignorant—of the suffering that rages outside. However, their illusion of safety is shattered when a mysterious, masked figure, personifying the Red Death, infiltrates their festivities and claims the lives of all within.

The enduring power of *The Masque of the Red Death* lies not merely in its haunting narrative but in the profound themes it explores: the arrogance of privilege, the inevitability of death, and the illusion of control. Poe's tale transcends its historical and cultural context, speaking to universal human fears and the unrelenting truth that no amount of wealth, power, or isolation can ward off mortality. Through his brilliant fusion of symbolism, setting, and psychological tension, Poe crafts a story that resonates with readers across generations, inviting reflection on the fragility of human existence.

The Gothic atmosphere of the story is established immediately, with vivid descriptions of the Red Death's symptoms—a grotesque plague that leaves victims covered in blood and causes death within minutes. The horror of the disease is not merely physical but also symbolic, representing both societal decay and the unstoppable force of time. Poe juxtaposes this outside horror with the artificial, almost decadent world that Prospero constructs within his castle. Here, color plays a significant role, especially in the sequence of seven colored rooms through which the masqueraders pass. These rooms, culminating in the ominous black chamber with its blood-red windows, represent the stages of life, with the final room symbolizing death. This progression transforms the castle into a metaphysical stage where the human journey from birth to death is enacted, culminating in the inevitable confrontation with mortality.

Poe's attention to detail, particularly in his use of color, architecture, and sound, deepens the allegorical resonance of the tale. The chiming of the ebony clock, which interrupts the revelry every hour, serves as a memento mori—a stark reminder of the passage of time and the approach of death. Each pause in the music, each moment of unease among the guests, heightens the tension and underscores the futility of their attempts to ignore their mortality. This interplay between sound, silence, and narrative progression creates a rhythm that mirrors the heartbeat of life itself, drawing the reader inexorably toward the story's chilling conclusion.

Themes of Privilege, Isolation, and Inevitability

At its core, *The Masque of the Red Death* is a critique of the belief that wealth and power can shield individuals from life's ultimate truths. Prince Prospero's actions—retreating from the plague and surrounding himself with luxury—reflect a broader commentary on the arrogance of those who imagine they can escape suffering by withdrawing from society. His masquerade ball, with its hedonistic revelry, serves as a metaphor for humanity's tendency to distract itself from the realities of death through pleasure, artifice, and denial. Yet, the arrival of the masked figure reminds us that no wall, no gate, and no amount of gold can keep death at bay.

The character of Prospero is particularly significant. Unlike the heroic princes of traditional fairy tales, he is neither noble nor compassionate. His name, which means "prosperous" or "fortunate," is laden with irony. His attempt to dominate and outwit death is not an act of courage but of hubris, and his eventual downfall serves as a moral lesson on the limits of human power. Poe's portrayal of Prospero's court, with its shallow amusements and gaudy displays of wealth, suggests a deeper critique of a society that turns inward during times of collective suffering, choosing self-indulgence over empathy and solidarity.

The mysterious figure of the Red Death is both literal and symbolic. It is described as a spectral intruder wearing a costume that mirrors the appearance of a corpse afflicted by the plague. The terror it evokes among the guests is not just due to its gruesome appearance but also because it embodies the inescapable truth they have sought to avoid. The figure's silent movement through the rooms mirrors the silent, invisible march of death itself—unseen, unpredictable, and unstoppable. When Prospero confronts this intruder, he discovers that it is not a mortal being but death personified, rendering his defiance meaningless.

Another key element of the story's symbolism is the aforementioned sequence of colored rooms. Scholars have long debated their meaning, but most interpretations agree that they represent the stages of human life. Starting with the blue room (associated with birth) and progressing through colors like purple, green, orange, white, and violet, the sequence ends in the black room, signifying the darkness of death. The guests' movement through these rooms during the masquerade is symbolic of the passage of time, a journey they cannot halt or reverse. The black room, with its blood-red windows and the looming ebony clock, serves as a grim reminder of the end that awaits all living beings.

The ebony clock itself is another powerful symbol. Its hourly chimes interrupt the music and dancing, momentarily freezing the revelers as they contemplate, however briefly, the passage of time. The clock thus functions as a narrative heartbeat, marking the relentless progression toward the story's climax. When the final stroke of midnight rings, it heralds not only the arrival of the Red Death but also the ultimate realization that time and mortality are the great equalizers.

Poe's Style and the Reader's Experience

Edgar Allan Poe's mastery of language and narrative structure is on full display in *The Masque of the Red Death*. His prose is both lyrical and precise, employing rich sensory imagery to create a sense of both beauty and dread. The lavish descriptions of the masquerade—the costumes, the music, the candlelit corridors—are interwoven with sinister undertones, creating a tension between surface pleasure and underlying horror. This juxtaposition mirrors the psychological state of the revelers, who strive to maintain an atmosphere of festivity even as they sense the encroaching threat of death.

Poe's use of allegory invites readers to engage with the story on multiple levels. On one hand, it is a straightforward Gothic tale of terror, with a mysterious intruder and a grim, inevitable conclusion. On the other hand, it is a philosophical meditation on mortality, time, and the human condition. Readers are encouraged to see themselves in the characters of Prospero and his guests—individuals who, like all of us, seek to deny the inevitability of death, yet who are ultimately powerless before it.

One of the most remarkable aspects of *The Masque of the Red Death* is its brevity. In just a few pages, Poe constructs an entire symbolic universe, filled with meaning and atmosphere. This economy of language is a hallmark of his style, enabling him to create maximum impact with minimal narrative scaffolding. Every detail—from the color of the rooms to the chiming of the clock—is imbued with significance, encouraging readers to contemplate the layers of meaning behind the imagery.

For modern readers, the story resonates in profound ways, especially in the wake of global pandemics and collective crises. The themes of isolation, privilege, and the futile attempt to escape death feel as urgent today as they did in the 19th century. The image of elites locking themselves away while a plague ravages the outside world serves as a stark reminder of the enduring social and moral divides that surface in times of disaster. Yet, as Poe demonstrates, no amount of privilege can provide true sanctuary from the universal fate that binds all humanity.

As you approach *The Masque of the Red Death*, it is worth reflecting on both its historical context and its timeless message. Written during an era when disease outbreaks were common and medical science was still limited, the story captures the fear and uncertainty that accompanied such crises. At the same time, its allegorical depth ensures that it speaks to readers far beyond its original time and place. Whether read as a Gothic horror story, a meditation on mortality, or a critique of social excess, Poe's tale offers an experience that is both intellectually stimulating and emotionally haunting.

The Masque of the Red Death

The "Red Death" had ravaged the country for a long time. No plague had ever been so deadly or so terrifying. Blood served as both its symbol and its mark—the crimson color and the terror of blood. Victims experienced sharp pains and sudden dizziness, followed by heavy bleeding from their pores, leading to death. The red marks that appeared on the body, particularly on the victim's face, acted as a curse that isolated them from any help or compassion from other people. The entire onset, development, and end of the disease occurred within just thirty minutes.

But Prince Prospero was happy, fearless, and wise. When half the people in his kingdom had died, he called together a thousand healthy and cheerful friends from among the knights and ladies of his court, and with them withdrew to the deep isolation of one of his fortified monasteries. This was a vast and magnificent building, created according to the prince's own unusual but impressive taste. A strong and high wall surrounded it completely. This wall had iron gates. After the courtiers had entered, they brought furnaces and heavy hammers and welded the locks shut. They decided to leave no way for anyone to enter or leave, preventing any sudden acts of desperation or madness from within. The monastery was well-stocked with supplies. With these precautions, the courtiers could defy the plague. The outside world could look after itself. Meanwhile, it would be foolish to mourn or to worry. The prince had supplied everything needed for enjoyment. There were jesters, there were improvisers, there were ballet dancers, there were musicians, there was beauty, there was wine. All of these things and safety were inside. Outside was the "Red Death".

It was near the end of the fifth or sixth month of his isolation, and while the plague was spreading most violently outside, that Prince Prospero hosted his thousand friends at a masquerade ball of extraordinary splendor.

It was a luxurious scene, that masquerade. But first let me describe the rooms where it took place. There were seven of them—a magnificent suite. In most palaces, such suites create a long, straight view, with folding doors that slide back almost to the walls on both sides, so you can see the entire length without obstruction. Here the situation was completely different, which you might expect given the duke's passion for the unusual. The rooms were arranged so irregularly that you could see little more than one room at a time. There was a sharp turn every twenty or thirty yards, and each turn created a new visual effect. On the right and left, in the center of each wall, a tall and narrow Gothic window looked out onto an enclosed hallway that followed the winding path of the suite. These windows were made of stained glass, and their colors matched the dominant shade of the decorations in the room they opened into. The one at the eastern end was decorated in blue—and its windows were brilliantly blue. The second room featured purple ornaments and tapestries, and here the window panes were purple. The third was green throughout, and so were the windows. The fourth was furnished and lit with orange—the fifth with white—the sixth with violet. The seventh room was completely covered in black velvet tapestries that hung across the entire ceiling and down the walls, falling in thick folds onto a carpet of the same material and color. But only in this room did the window color fail to match the decorations. The panes here were scarlet—a deep blood red. In none of the seven rooms was there any lamp or candelabra, despite the abundance of golden ornaments scattered about or hanging from the ceiling. No light of any kind came from lamps or candles within the suite of rooms. But in the hallways that ran alongside the suite, there stood opposite each window a heavy tripod holding a brazier of fire that cast its rays through the colored glass and brightly lit each room. This created a multitude of vivid and fantastical visual effects. But in the western or black room, the effect of the firelight streaming through the blood-colored panes onto the dark hangings was extremely ghastly, and created such a wild appearance on the faces of those who entered that few members of the party were brave enough to step foot inside its boundaries at all.

In this same room, there was also an enormous ebony clock standing against the western wall. Its pendulum swung back and forth with a dull, heavy, monotonous sound; and when the minute hand completed its circle around the face and the hour was about to strike, a sound emerged from the brass interior of the clock that was clear and loud and deep and extremely musical, but with such a strange tone and emphasis that, each time an hour passed, the orchestra musicians were forced to pause briefly in their performance to listen to the sound; and so the dancers had to stop their movements; and there was a momentary disruption of the entire cheerful gathering; and, while the clock's chimes still rang, it was noticed that even the most carefree grew pale, and the older and more serious guests passed their hands over their foreheads as if lost in confused thought or contemplation. But when the echoes had completely faded, light laughter immediately spread throughout the assembly; the musicians looked at each other and smiled as if at their own anxiety and foolishness, and made whispered promises to one another that the next chiming of the clock would not produce the same feeling in them; and then, after sixty minutes had passed, (which contains three thousand six hundred seconds of Time that flies,) there came another chiming of the clock, and then there was the same disruption and nervousness and contemplation as before.

Despite all of this, the celebration was joyful and spectacular. The duke had unusual tastes. He possessed an excellent sense of color and visual impact. He ignored the conventions of ordinary fashion. His designs were daring and passionate, and his ideas blazed with wild splendor. Some people might have considered him insane. His followers believed he was not. You had to listen to him, observe him, and be in his presence to be certain that he was not.

He had largely overseen the movable decorations of the seven rooms for this grand celebration, and it was his own refined taste that had shaped the character of the costumed guests. They were certainly grotesque. There was much brilliance and sparkle and sharpness and illusion—much of what would later be seen in "Hernani." There were ornate figures with mismatched limbs and accessories. There were wild fantasies like those a madman creates. There was much that was beautiful, much that was indulgent, much that was strange, something that was terrifying, and quite a bit that might have caused revulsion. Back and forth through the seven rooms there moved, in reality, a crowd of dreams. And these dreams twisted in and around, taking color from the rooms, and making the wild music of the orchestra seem like the echo of their footsteps. And then the ebony clock that stands in the hall of velvet strikes the hour. And for a moment, everything becomes still, and all is quiet except for the voice of the clock. The dreams freeze motionless where they stand. But the echoes of the chime fade away—they have lasted only an instant—and a soft, muted laughter drifts after them as they disappear. And now the music rises again, and the dreams come alive, and twist back and forth more cheerfully than before, taking color from the many-colored windows through which the light streams from the braziers. But into the chamber that lies furthest west of the seven, none of the masked figures now dare to venture; for the night is drawing to a close; and a deeper red light flows through the blood-colored glass; and the darkness of the black drapery frightens; and to anyone whose foot steps upon the black carpet, there comes from the nearby ebony clock a muffled toll more solemnly forceful than any sound that reaches the ears of those who enjoy the more distant festivities of the other rooms.

But these other rooms were packed with people, and in them the heart of life beat with feverish intensity. And the celebration continued in a whirling dance, until finally the clock began to strike midnight. And then the music stopped, as I have described; and the movements of the dancers came to a halt; and there was an uncomfortable pause in all activities as before. But now there were twelve chimes to be struck by the clock's bell; and so it occurred, perhaps, that deeper thoughts crept, with the passage of time, into the contemplations of the more reflective among those who were celebrating. And so it also occurred, perhaps, that before the final echoes of the last chime had completely faded into silence, there were many people in the crowd who had found time to notice the presence of a masked figure that had not caught anyone's attention before. And the whispered rumors of this new presence having spread throughout the gathering, there eventually arose from the entire company a buzzing sound, or murmur, expressing disapproval and surprise—then, finally, terror, horror, and disgust.

In a gathering of illusions like the one I have described, you might expect that no ordinary sight could have caused such a reaction. The truth was that the masquerade's freedom that night was almost without limits; but this particular figure had exceeded all bounds, going far beyond even the prince's loose standards of acceptable behavior. There are certain feelings in the hearts of even the most reckless people that cannot be stirred without causing deep emotion. Even among those who are completely lost, for whom life and death are nothing but jokes, there are some things that cannot be made into a joke. The entire group of guests now seemed to feel deeply that the stranger's costume and manner showed neither cleverness nor appropriateness. The figure was tall and thin, covered from head to toe in burial clothes. The mask that hid the face was made to look so much like the face of a rigid corpse that even the closest examination would have struggled to spot the deception. And yet all of this might have been tolerated, if not welcomed, by the wild party-goers around him. But this costumed figure had gone so far as to take on the appearance of the Red Death itself. His clothing was stained with blood—and his wide forehead, along with all his facial features, was splattered with the scarlet terror.

When Prince Prospero's eyes landed on this ghostly figure (which moved slowly and solemnly among the dancers, as if deliberately playing its part to the fullest) he visibly shook with what seemed to be either fear or revulsion; but immediately after, his face flushed red with anger.

"Who dares," he demanded in a harsh voice to the courtiers standing nearby, "who dares to insult us with this sacrilegious mockery? Grab him and remove his mask so we can find out who we need to hang from the castle walls at sunrise!"

Prince Prospero stood in the eastern chamber, the blue one, when he spoke these words. His voice echoed loudly and clearly through all seven rooms, since the prince was a bold and strong man, and the music had fallen silent when he raised his hand.

The prince stood in the blue room, surrounded by a group of pale courtiers. When he first spoke, there was a slight rushing movement from this group toward the intruder, who was also nearby at that moment and now approached the speaker with deliberate and stately steps. However, because of a certain indescribable fear that the mad behavior of the masked figure had inspired in the entire party, no one was found who would reach out to seize him. So, without obstruction, he passed within a yard of the prince's position. While the vast assembly, as if moved by a single impulse, shrank from the centers of the rooms toward the walls, he made his way without interruption, maintaining the same solemn and measured pace that had marked him from the beginning, through the blue chamber to the purple—through the purple to the green—through the green to the orange—through this again to the white—and even from there to the violet, before any decisive movement had been made to stop him. It was then, however, that Prince Prospero, driven mad with rage and shame at his own momentary cowardice, rushed hastily through the six chambers, while no one followed him because of a deadly terror that had gripped them all. He carried a drawn dagger held high, and had approached with rapid force to within three or four feet of the retreating figure, when the latter, having reached the far end of the velvet apartment, suddenly turned and faced his pursuer. There was a sharp cry—and the dagger fell gleaming onto the black carpet, upon which, immediately afterward, Prince Prospero collapsed dead. Then, summoning the wild courage born of desperation, a crowd of the party-goers immediately rushed into the black apartment and, grabbing the masked figure whose tall form stood upright and motionless within the shadow of the ebony clock, gasped in unspeakable horror to discover that the grave clothes and corpse-like mask, which they handled with such violent roughness, contained no tangible form whatsoever.

Now everyone recognized that the Red Death was among them. It had arrived like a thief in the night. One by one, the party guests collapsed in the blood-stained halls where they had been celebrating, and each person died in the desperate position where they had fallen. The life of the black clock ended along with the last of the cheerful revelers. The flames of the tripods went out. And Darkness and

Decay and the Red Death ruled without limits over everything.

THE END

Thank You For Reading

You've Just Read a Piece of the Greatest Library Ever Rebuilt

Thank you for reading.

This book is one of thousands we're restoring, reimagining, and translating as part of the **Modern Library of Alexandria** — a global movement to preserve and share humanity's most important ideas.

What was once lost to fire and time is now rising again — not just as memory, but as living, breathing knowledge, freely accessible to all.

What You Can Do Next:

* **Keep Reading.**

  Discover more legendary works — in beautiful print, audiobook, or digital form — at LibraryofAlexandria.com.

* **Build Your Own Library.**

  Every title is available as a paperback, hardcover, or collectible boxset — at true printing cost. Craft a personal library worthy of display.

* **Spread the Light.**

  Share this book. Tell others about the movement. Help us translate every timeless work into every language, so no reader is ever left behind.

By finishing this book, you've already taken part in something extraordinary.

Join us at LibraryofAlexandria.com

Together, we're rebuilding the greatest library the world has ever known.

With appreciation,

The Modern Library of Alexandria Team

Visit:
www.libraryofalexandria.com
Or scan the code below: